The Sweetest Scoop

Ben & Jerry's Ice Cream Revolution

Words by
LISA ROBINSON

Pictures by
STACY INNERST

ABRAMS BOOKS FOR YOUNG READERS
NEW YORK

Close your eyes and imagine holding an ice cream cone.

Now take a lick . . .
What does it taste like?
Chocolate, vanilla, strawberry?
A cool swim on a hot summer day?

What about Wavy Gravy,
Truffle Kerfuffle,
or Chubby Hubby?

What's the scoop on
those wacky flavors?!

Let's find out . . .

It all began in 1963.

As luck would have it, two groovy guys, Ben Cohen and Jerry Greenfield, met when they were twelve years old.

Although Ben liked art and Jerry liked science, they still found
lots to do together. They tooled around on bikes, camped out,
and scarfed down slice after slice at Sam and Tony's pizza parlor.
Ben and Jerry loved all kinds of food . . . especially ice cream!

One summer, they figured out how to mix
ice cream, fun, and making a buck.
Ben drove an ice cream truck and Jerry
came along for the ride, scooping the
ice cream and telling goofy jokes.

After high school, they went their separate ways. Ben dropped out of college to become a potter. No one bought his teapots.

Jerry finished college and wanted to become a doctor. Every medical school he applied to rejected him.

Defeated and discouraged, they met up in New York City to brainstorm what to do next. If they started a business together, they'd be their own bosses. And they'd make it fun!

What did they love to do most? Eat!

They rustled up a plan for a bagel delivery business.

Every Sunday morning, customers would receive bagels, cream cheese, lox, and a *New York Times*. They'd call it UBS: United Bagel Service. Except ... they didn't have enough money to buy bagel-making equipment. Foiled!

Everything You Need to Know About Making ICE CREAM
*not bagels

What do ghosts put on their bagels? **Scream cheese!**

But Ben and Jerry didn't give up. They loved ice cream, too, so they read a book about how to make it. Good news— ice cream was cheaper to make than bagels. Sweet!

Next, they whipped up a list of places to open a shop. Since students love ice cream, they searched for college towns. Burlington, Vermont, had four colleges—and zero ice cream shops. Perfect!

They rented an abandoned gas station. The roof leaked, ice coated the floor, and the toilets were broken.

So they patched the roof,

fixed the heat,

and called a plumber . . .

but they didn't have
enough money to pay
the plumber. Then Jerry
had a brilliant idea . . .

…offer the plumber membership to the
Ice Cream for Life Club as payment!

Ben pointed out that there wasn't an Ice Cream for Life Club.
So they started one. The plumber happily joined. Do you want
to be a member of the Ice Cream for Life Club? Me, too!

Next, they had to solve a bigger problem: how to actually *make ice cream*.
Teamwork was the answer. Jerry, the scientist, experimented with cream,
milk, sugar, and eggs for the ice cream base.

Ben, the artist, crafted clever combinations of chocolate, caramel, and cookies.

How do you make a milkshake?
Give a cow a pogo stick!

After a few failures and lots of taste testing, they created a formula for the kind of ice cream they wanted: rich, creamy, and chewy. Seems like a yummy job, doesn't it?

BEN & JERRY'

Finally, on May 5, 1978,
the doors of Ben & Jerry's
Homemade ice cream shop opened.
And people came. *Lots* of people!

HOMEMADE

But there were still some bumps on the road ahead...

Why did the ice cream truck break down? **Because of the rocky road!**

For example, how could they make lots and lots of Coffee Toffee Bar Crunch if they had to cut the toffee bars one by one?

Chop.

Chop.

Chop...

It took forever to get through a twenty-pound box!

Frustrated, Jerry hurled a box to the ground.

SMASH!

The bars broke into
just-the-right-size pieces!
From then on, they climbed
a six-foot ladder and flung
the boxes to the floor.
(Don't try this at home!)

Toffee

Toffee

Toffee

And still more challenges churned their way—like how to make their flavors stand out. There were already so many kinds of ice cream for sale! What if they dreamed up fabulous flavors with cool names, like Chunky Monkey, Phish Food, and Dastardly Mash?

They welcomed customers' ideas, too. An anonymous postcard arrived suggesting "Cherry Garcia," named after a popular musician, Jerry Garcia. The cherry ice cream with fudge flakes quickly became a hit.

Some flavors flopped, though, like Sugar Plum, a mix of plum and caramel ice cream. Or Oh Pear, pear ice cream with almond and fudge. And Peanut Butter and Jelly, peanut butter ice cream with strawberry jelly swirl. But by now, Ben and Jerry knew how to face failure: First and foremost, stir up a silly solution.

And so, to honor and remember dearly departed flavors, they opened the Flavor Graveyard. Epitaphs commemorate Bovinity Divinity, Fossil Fuel, Vermonty Python, and many more.

But then, just when they thought everything was chill ...

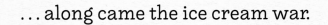
. . . along came the ice cream war.

Pillsbury, a big food company,
threatened to remove its ice cream from
stores that sold Ben & Jerry's. The
stores panicked and refused to stock
their shelves with Ben & Jerry's ice
cream. Ben & Jerry's was blocked!

Once again, it was time to get creative—and get a little help from their friends.

Their SOS message appeared everywhere:

buses,

plane banners,

billboards,

and bumper stickers.

F.T.C.

Thousands of loyal customers protested the blockade.
They called and wrote letters to the Federal Trade
Commission. Finally, Pillsbury backed down.
And Ben and Jerry returned to selling their
ice cream throughout New England.

By 1987, ice cream lovers could find Ben & Jerry's
ice cream in stores all over the United States.

But Ben and Jerry wanted to do more. They'd grown up during the 1960s, a time of turmoil and change, as people marched in the streets demanding civil rights for all and an end to war. These causes mattered to Ben and Jerry. And they believed they could use ice cream to help make the world a better place.

Why not start with their employees? They paid them well. They invited them to bring their dogs to work. And every day, workers took home free ice cream.

Next came the factory and its effect on the environment. Bleaching paper for ice cream packaging releases chlorine, a harmful chemical, into local water supplies. So Ben and Jerry invented a carton that doesn't do that. They also looked for other ways to make ice cream that don't hurt the planet, like reducing waste and using solar panels for electricity.

But they wanted to think even bigger. They decided to donate profits to causes they cared about. Playful ice cream flavors would spread the word: Save Our Swirled to promote awareness of climate change; Imagine Whirled Peace to demand an end to war; I Dough, I Dough to support same-sex marriage; and Empower Mint to call attention to the unfairness of the growing gap between rich and poor.

Finally, they formed the Ben & Jerry's Foundation to support "social and environmental justice around the country." More than twenty years later, the foundation is still going strong.

So the next time you enjoy a cone of Ben & Jerry's ice cream, you'll know that it's made of a lot more than cream and sugar.

And that one lick at a time, you, too, can dream of making the world a better place.

Now *that's* sweet!

Author's Note

I love ice cream, too! One cold February day, I drove my family to Waterbury, Vermont, to visit the Ben & Jerry's ice cream factory. As soon as we walked through the front door, we smelled the delicious scent of cream and sugar. On the tour, we saw how they make the ice cream: The Blend Tank mixes the cream, milk, sugar, and eggs; the Chunk Feeder folds in the nuts, cookies, and candies; and the Automatic Filler squirts the ice cream into cartons. Best of all, the tour ends in the Tasting Room, where you can sample a flavor or two.

It wasn't just the yummy ice cream that drew me to writing about Ben and Jerry, though. What made me realize that this is an important story to tell was Ben and Jerry's creative and persistent pursuit of their dream and their commitment to social and environmental justice.

Can ice cream make the world a better place? Ben and Jerry think so. They believe that social activism is a responsibility of individuals and businesses. Social activism means taking action to bring about political or social change; activists are people who work to make these changes. They often fight for social justice: fairness and equal opportunities for everyone, no matter their skin color, gender, sexuality, ethnicity, religion, physical ability, or age. In 2000, when Ben and Jerry sold their business to Unilever, a large corporation, they insisted that Unilever continue to support the causes and ideals that mattered to them. Unilever agreed to continue Ben & Jerry's social mission.

In 2020, in response to increasing national awareness about and protesting against police brutality against Black people, Ben & Jerry's released a corporate statement that serves as a strong example of how big corporations can use their power to advance social justice. The statement asked President Trump to cease racist comments in order to promote healing, recommended that Congress work toward making reparations for slavery, supported legislation for police accountability, and suggested a revitalization of the Civil Rights Division of the Justice Department.

I hope Ben and Jerry's story inspires you to follow your dreams, even if you find yourself on a rocky road. *And* to find ways to give back to your community on the journey.

 **Timeline**

March 14, 1951   Jerry Greenfield's birthday*

March 18, 1951   Ben Cohen's birthday*

Ben and Jerry were born in the same hospital four days apart, but didn't meet until twelve years later!

1963   Ben and Jerry meet in junior high school on Long Island, New York.

1969   Ben and Jerry graduate high school.

1972   Ben drops out of Colgate University.

1973   Jerry graduates from Oberlin College.

1977   Ben and Jerry move to Burlington, Vermont, and rent a gas station for their shop.

1978   Ben & Jerry's Homemade ice cream shop opens.

1979   First Free Cone Day, an annual event that still continues today.

1980   Ben and Jerry rent an old spool and bobbin factory so they can package ice cream into pints for sale.

1984   Pillsbury blocks New England stores from selling Ben & Jerry's ice cream.

1985   The Ben & Jerry's Foundation begins.

1987   **New flavor alert!** Cherry Garcia is born—it's still a bestseller today!

1987   Ben & Jerry's wins the court case against Pillsbury's unfair trade practices. All stores in America can sell their ice cream. Ben & Jerry's ice cream becomes available throughout the United States.

1989 **New Flavor Alert!** Sugar Plum, plum ice cream with a caramel swirl, lasts only a year before it is sent to the flavor graveyard.

1991 **New Flavor Alert!** Chocolate Chip Cookie Dough appears and becomes a bestseller.

2000 Ben and Jerry sell their business to Unilever, a multinational food corporation.

2007 **New Flavor Alert!** Imagine Whirled Peace honors musician John Lennon and promotes world peace. A portion of the proceeds go to the Peace One Day foundation.

2009 **New Flavor Alert!** The company renames a flavor, Yes, Pecan, to honor President Obama's presidential victory and pledges to donate all proceeds to the Common Cause Education Fund.

2015 **New flavor Alert!** I Dough, I Dough celebrates the Supreme Court's decision to guarantee the right to same-sex marriage throughout the United States. All proceeds go to the Human Rights Campaign's LGBTQ+ equal rights advocacy.

2016 Ben & Jerry's releases several flavors of vegan, non-dairy ice cream: Chunky Monkey, Chocolate Fudge Brownie, P.B. & Cookies, and Coffee Caramel Fudge.

2019 **New Flavor Alert!** Justice ReMix'd calls attention to problems with racism in the criminal justice system. Proceeds go to the Advancement Project, a civil rights organization dedicated to promoting a caring, inclusive, and just democracy.

2020 In response to police violence toward Black people, Ben & Jerry's issues a powerful corporate statement in support of the Black Lives Matter movement that demands the dismantling of white supremacy in America.

2020 **New Flavor Alert!** Change the Whirled, a non-dairy ice cream, celebrates vegan football player Colin Kaepernick for taking a knee to protest police brutality and racism. Proceeds go to the Know Your Rights Camp, an organization Kaepernick founded to empower Black and Brown youth.

Sources

Ben & Jerry's. "Flavor Graveyard." Accessed February 2, 2021. See www.benjerry.com/flavors/flavor-graveyard.

Ben & Jerry's. "Socially Responsible Causes Ben & Jerry's Has Advocated For." Accessed February 2, 2021. See www.benjerry.com/whats-new/2014/corporate-social-responsibility-history.

Egessa, Patricia. "How Ben & Jerry's Took on Pillsbury and Won." *Innovations Online*, November 7, 2016. See innovationsjournal.net/how-ben-jerrys-took-on-pillsbury-and-won-13959a83730e.

Gelles, David. "How the Social Mission of Ben & Jerry's Survived Being Gobbled Up." *New York Times*, August 21, 2015. See www.nytimes.com/2015/08/23/business/how-ben-jerrys-social-mission-survived-being-gobbled-up.html.

Lager, Fred. *Ben & Jerry's: The Inside Scoop: How Two Real Guys Built a Business with Social Conscience and a Sense of Humor.* New York: Crown Publishers, 1994.

New York Times. "Vermont's Ice Cream Upstart." *New York Times*, March 29, 1985. See www.nytimes.com/1985/03/29/business/vermont-s-ice-cream-upstart.html.

Packaging Network. "Ben & Jerry's Switches to Unbleached Paperboard Ice Cream Pint." Accessed February 2, 2021. See www.packagingnetwork.com/doc/ben-jerrys-switches-to-unbleached-paperboard-0001.

Raz, Guy. "Ben & Jerry's: Ben Cohen and Jerry Greenfield." Interview by Guy Raz. *How I Built This with Guy Raz*, NPR One, November 20, 2017. See one.npr.org/i/562899429:564777542.

Shapiro, Annie. "The Inside Scoop on Ben & Jerry's Unique Company Culture." *Namely*, July 27, 2017. See blog.namely.com/blog/ben-jerrys-unique-company-culture.

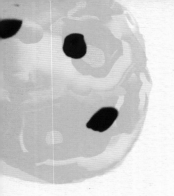

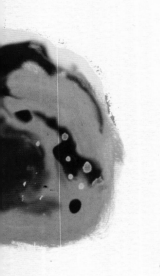

For Alyssa Eisner Henkin,
who gave me the sweet suggestion for this story
—L.R.

For Susan

—S.I.

The illustrations for this book were made with watercolor, ink, and Photoshop.

Cataloging-in-Publication Data has been applied for and
may be obtained from the Library of Congress.

ISBN 978-1-4197-4803-5

Text © 2022 Lisa Robinson
Illustrations © 2022 Stacy Innerst
Book design by Heather Kelly

Printed and bound in China
10 9 8 7 6 5 4 3 2

Abrams Books for Young Readers are available at special discounts when purchased in quantity
for premiums and promotions as well as fundraising or educational use. Special editions can also be created
to specification. For details, contact specialsales@abramsbooks.com or the address below.

Abrams® is a registered trademark of Harry N. Abrams, Inc.

ABRAMS The Art of Books
195 Broadway, New York, NY 10007
abramsbooks.com

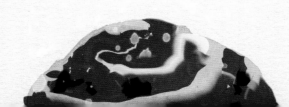